2/01
7.95

WHAT'S IN THE TIDE POOL?

By Anne Hunter

Houghton Mifflin Company
Boston 2000

What's in the tide pool?

Periwinkles

Periwinkles are small snails that live between the low and high tide zones. They travel slowly on their snail foot, feeding at high tide on the algae growing on the tide pool rocks. When the tide is out, periwinkles retreat into their shells and are capable of surviving for hours without water, closed away from the drying air. They measure about an inch long.

A Ruddy Turnstone

The ruddy turnstone is a stout sandpiper that stops at the tide pool on its journey between its summer nesting place in the northern tundra and its wintering ground in the far south. It picks through the seaweed and turns over small stones at the tidepool's edge to feed on snails and small sea animals. Its call is a series of low, rattling whistles. Ruddy turnstones measure nine and a half inches long.

A Blue Mussel

Blue mussels often live in colonies attached to the rocks in the intertidal zone. Mussels are a type of bivalve, which is a creature whose shell has two hinged halves, or valves. They feed by filtering seawater through gills to strain out algae and plankton. Blue mussels can measure up to four inches long.

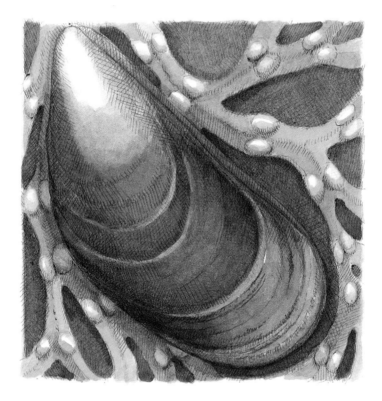

A SEA ANEMONE

There are many kinds of sea anemones living under the water, attached to rocks in the tide pool. Anemones use their tentacles to capture and eat small fish, shrimp, and other creatures brought in on the tide. Their tentacles retract instantly when threatened, making them less visible. The sea anemone measures two to four inches high.

A GREEN CRAB

Many different kinds of crabs live in tide pools. The green crab lives under the seaweed and rocks, using its large front claws to scavenge. It helps to keep the tidal area clean of dead fish and other decaying creatures. Green crabs walk sideways on their four pairs of legs. They grow to over three inches wide.

BARNACLES

Barnacles live in colonies attached to rocks in the tide pool. When the tide is high, barnacles feed by brushing the water with delicate, fanlike feet, filtering tiny plants and animals called plankton. At low tide, barnacles close the plates at the top of their cone-shaped shell, protecting their bodies from the drying air. Of the many kinds of barnacles, most measure from a quarter inch to an inch high and wide.

A Sea Star

There are many varieties of sea stars, or starfish, that move slowly over the floor of the tide pool. Most have five legs, covered on the bottoms with many feet tipped with suction cups, used to anchor themselves to the sea floor. They also use these feet to pry open the shells of clams and mussels, which they devour with a mouth located at the center of their underside. The northern sea star can grow to six inches across.

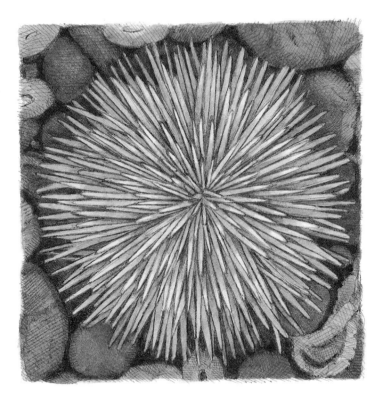

A HERMIT CRAB

The hermit crab scuttles along the bottom of the tide pool, wearing a discarded snail shell on its soft, vulnerable abdomen. As the hermit crab grows, it must move into a larger shell. Like most crabs, hermit crabs are scavengers, feeding on dead creatures. Most hermit crabs grow to three-quarters of an inch long.

Looking into a tide pool is like peering into a treasure box, rich with color and detail. Tide pools hold a wealth of life, and their seemingly delicate creatures can withstand extreme conditions, from drying air and sun at low tide to pounding waves. Although tide pool dwellers are equipped to survive waves and sun, they have poor defenses against human feet. Be careful where you step. If you watch, as quiet and still as the rocks around you, the exotic life below the surface will slowly emerge.